Dedication

This book is dedicated to my wife Beth Bland and my children Joshua, Christopher and Jessica who inspire me more than they will ever know.

Contents

#1) You are responsible for your own happiness.

#2) You are always either moving towards your goals… or you are drifting away.

#3) You can't change anyone but yourself.

#4) Learn to be thankful. We all have reasons to be grateful.

#5) We are not solitary creatures. We all need good friendships.

#6) Don't wait for permission to live.

#7) Never waste a minute bemoaning getting older.

#8) Stop worrying about what other people think of you.

#9) Have standards. They must be yours or they are of little value.

#10) The only thing you can always have control over is your attitude.

#11) Avoid making your identity your career or your possessions.

#12) Forgiving those who wrong you is the gift you give yourself.

#13) Never pretend to be what others want you to be.

#14) Jealousy is the crystal meth of the soul.

#15) Money may not buy you happiness, but the lack of it can ruin your whole day.

#16) Happiness is not a destination, but the journey of a lifetime.

#17) Be your own best friend. Accept yourself.

#18) It's sharper than any two edged sword…tame your tongue.

#19) Put your mind on a diet. Stay away from the evening news.

#20) Hope is the ship that carries the soul. It is impossible to be happy without it.

#21) Music can restore the soul and bring joy to the heart.

#22) If laughter is the best medicine, then take two jokes and call me…

#23) Avoid needless confrontation over small matters with petty people.

#24) Indecision is the enemy of happiness. Make a decision, and be happy.

#25) You can't please everyone. Set boundaries and learn the word "No."

#26) You can't make a good deal with a bad person.

#27) Whistle while you work, but work.

#28) Sometimes the members of our family have tails.

#29) In life you get what you are willing to settle for.

#30) Never stop learning. It will expand your mind and your opportunities.

#31) True lifelong happiness will only find you when you find your life's calling.

#32) It's hard to be happy when you're flabby…

#33) The main ingredient in the recipe of a happy life is balance.

#34) No man succeeds alone…ask for help.

#35) The golden nuggets of life are not yielded to the lazy. Be persistent.

#36) Two are better than one…love may be life's true treasure hunt.

#37) Like rain clouds on a summer's day…disappointment can cast a shadow…

#38) Teach what you know, share what you love.

#39) Put your stamp on the world. Create and be creative.

#40) The only thing worse than lending money…is to borrow from them.

#41) A little ink saves a lot of grief.

#42) Take a break. Change your scenery. Re-energize your body mind and soul.

#43) Live below your means. Avoid credit and pay cash.

#44) Be open to learn, but stay true to yourself while dealing with a critical world.

#45) Do what is right. You will create a happiness you can live with.

#46) Your subconscious is always listening. It believes everything.

#47) Just like your mom said, "go outside and play."

#48) Happiness is not complete when you don't know God. You need to know him.

THE LAWS OF HAPPINESS

Man has been seeking happiness in some form since the beginning of time. It means different things to different people. Some believe money will make them happy. For others it's being with that certain person, achieving a goal or a desired status. So why do so many successful people find themselves unhappy and how can you become a happier person?

This is the mystery. What does it take to make a happy person and how do we avoid the triggers that can lead to depression?

Mental health issues have, in the last ten years, stepped out of the shadows and have become something millions of Americans deal with on a daily basis. Drugs are often given to treat depression and to stabilize mood swings. The warnings on some of the very medications we give to the depressed include: "Increased thoughts of suicide." It is alarming how many people each day are prescribed antidepressants. This is not to say that medication should never be used, some people are truly clinically depressed while others may only be unhappy. In any case the laws of happiness found in this book will highlight the truths that can and *will* make you a happier person, if followed, and will help your friends and family too.

In the following pages I will share each of the 48 laws, which I have researched and more importantly lived over the past fifty-two years. These laws are truths; they are golden nuggets, time tested and proven to create a happier life. Each law is explained with real life examples, historical facts and stories. As you read, the mystery of happiness will be revealed.

LAW #1

You are responsible for your own happiness. No one can give it to you or completely take it away.

When we wait for others to make us happy it is unreliable at best and disappointing at worst. Not only is it unfair to expect that much from anyone, but you set them up for failure. No one wants to be responsible for your happiness. They want to enjoy your company and celebrate in all the good things you bring to the relationship. If you put such a large expectation on those in your life and they let you down (which they will) you have now gained a new problem; resentment. We all know people we avoid in social settings. They are so empty and in need of attention that they will suck you dry if you let them. Their desperation creates the very loneliness they seek to quench. This is not what you want.

It is up to you to learn what and how to be happy. Do not make excuses. Don't be afraid to really look at your life and see what needs changing. If you master how to be happy, you can take all the pressure off of those around you and become someone who has something to contribute.

If you take responsibility for your own happiness you will be more resilient when bad things happen. Not to say things can't get you down from time to time, but you will have the tools to adjust to even devastating events. Consider Joni Eareckson Tada. She was a young girl of seventeen in 1967 when a diving accident left her a quadriplegic in a wheelchair unable to use her legs or arms. She had very different plans for her life. She was now faced with the same question each of us face every day, what will I do with my life? What *can* I do with my life? She could have sat in that chair and blamed God. She could have felt sorry for herself. No one would have blamed her. But she wanted to live. She wanted her life to count for something. Isn't that what we all want? She learned to paint holding the brush with her teeth. She made beautiful paintings that sold. She wrote a book that was a best seller. She became a public speaker. I saw Joni speak in 1978 in Anaheim, California. She was surprisingly powerful for a young woman sitting so still in that wheelchair. I remember thinking, "What do I have to complain about in my life?" I admired her resolve. Joni went on to speak in over forty-six different counties. She has had her own radio broadcast and she got married. Joni overcame tragedy and found happiness while making a difference. So can you.

"Happiness depends upon ourselves."
Aristotle (384 bc-322 b.c.) Greek philosopher

LAW #2

You are always either moving towards your goals, relationships and abilities or you are drifting away. You are never truly standing still.

We all know people who dabble, trying at this or that, never really committing to anything. All the while never understanding why they can't seem to get anywhere. So it goes with your goals and talents. You may be endowed with certain gifts: a great voice, a strong pitching arm, a sharp mind, something unique to you. But as naturally talented as you may be, without hard persistent work at developing that ability you will never be able to enjoy your true potential. Unrealized potential can leave you with an emptiness that can follow you for years. So find what you're good at and work at it. Don't put off becoming great. Steady effort will yield life changing results. Refrain from starting and stopping over and over again. It's like a man who swims against the tide. He swims for awhile, floats, swims, floats and swims again; always having to cover the same distance never arriving at the shore.

It is easy to take relationships for granted. Just look at the divorce rate. Today people have such busy lives raising the kids, paying the rent and building the career. Sometimes along the way we can lose sight of the most important relationship we have, our spouse. We may stop doing the things that caused our mate to fall in love with us back in the beginning. My wife, Beth, and I have been married for twenty-seven years. In our first few years we had two small children that took just about everything out of us (as small children do). It seemed every conversation we had was about the kids or some bill to pay. I felt we had lost a lot of why we got married in the first place. We were both so busy "*doing*" that we stopped "*being*" a couple. So we established a date night. Every Thursday night we got a babysitter and went to dinner or a movie or took a drive. The only rule was we couldn't talk about the kids. It forced us to reconnect. I didn't just love my wife; I was *in* love with her. It takes work to stay in love and it takes work to be lovable, but it is worth it.

The relationship with your kids takes every bit as much time and effort as any other relationship you may have and in many ways it is more important. You could be married more than once and have a few life partners, but you are the only father or mother your child will ever have. This is the most formative relationship in your child's life. More time has been racked up on a doctor's couch talking about a neglectful parent than any other topic. Kids need far more time than you might think. Dads model hard work, responsibility and strength for their sons. For their daughters, dads teach them how they should expect to be treated by a man. Daughters need dads to make them feel pretty, loved and treasured. Dads are not superfluous. Sons and daughters also need their moms. Boys learn how to treat women with love, kindness and respect. Moms help to civilize boys before they're let loose on the world. Girls are shown how to be a lady, how to wear makeup, do their hair and how to dress. Daughters also learn how to be self-sacrificing and giving. Many parents think because they spent last summer with their kids that they know them, but the truth is your kids change about every three months. Their friends change and so do their interests. In order to have the influence on them you want you must spend time with them. Take them on a drive, see a movie, or spend the day fishing. The more you do with them the more opportunities you have to talk and listen, thus, you won't drift away.

"The man who is born with a talent which he was meant to use finds his greatest happiness in using it." Johann Wolfgang Von Goethe (1749-1832) German Poet.

LAW #3

You can't change others. You can persuade, teach, encourage, help and admonish, but you cannot change anyone but yourself.

A sure path to being unhappy is trying to change someone else. Yes, **trying** because you can't do it. It really is the height of arrogance to think you have that much power. Not even God can change someone who doesn't want to be changed. Often times a woman will find a man that is *almost* what she wants in a mate. "If he was just a little more like this or a little less like that, then he would be perfect," we've all heard something like this before. You only become frustrated and resentful when the person you seek to change remains the same. People can and do change for all sorts of reasons. Even as you read this book you may find things about yourself you might want to adjust. The book would be a type of persuasion. That's how we change. We find the need and the courage to leave behind what's not working and start down a new path. But change is not easy for most of us. My father was a good man, a hard working man. He worked for Weber's bakery for twenty-three years and only missed one day of work throughout his career there due to food poisoning. My father was also a terrible alcoholic. He would drink day in and day out.

He would fight with my mom then black out at night. I loved my dad, we all did, but as much as I wanted him to stop drinking I couldn't make him stop. A year after my mother died and two weeks after I was married, in the summer of 1984, my father drank himself to death. I couldn't change him.

The best use of your energy should be reserved for changing yourself. Lead by example and reap the rewards.

> "Happiness is not something readymade. It comes from your own actions."
> **Dalai Lama XIV**

LAW #4
Learn to be thankful. Spend time each day practicing the art of appreciation. We all have reasons to be grateful.

It has been said, "Happiness is not found in getting what you want, but in wanting what you have." I think you would agree that a grateful person is probably a happy person. If that is true, then learning to appreciate your friends and family may be a good start to becoming a happier person. You can always find those with more than you have, but you can also find whole countries much less fortunate than you. You have clean water, fresh food, a home, education, medicine and boundless opportunities all around you. Learning to reflect and show appreciation takes practice. We always seem to be moving so fast, trying to achieve our goals, we can lose sight of how important it is to give thanks for all that we have accomplished so far. This is not to say you shouldn't seek to better your life, nor is ambition the antithesis of gratitude. But demonstrating your gratitude toward others is every bit as vital as simply feeling grateful. Let the people in your life know how much they mean to you. Go out of your way for them. Give them a card or a small gift, something unexpected to show your appreciation. This will add value to your life far more than you may realize and more than any gift does for the receiver. Take time to be kind to those you come in contact with. It costs you nothing to give a smile and a kind word, but can add so much to those you give it to.

"Giving back," is when you take a small portion of your success and spend some of your time and resources to help those less fortunate than yourself. It could be volunteering at a soup kitchen or working with your church's youth group, it doesn't matter what it is, just give back.

"Let us be grateful to the people who make us happy; they are the charming gardeners who make our souls blossom."
Marcel Proust

LAW #5
We are not solitary creatures. We are social. We all need good friendships to magnify life's experiences.

No man is an island. We are all born needing interaction and connection with others. There was a famous experiment where they took four baby chimps, two of which were given love, attention and lots of contact. The other two were given food and water, but all love and contact was withheld. The first two thrived. The second pair barely gained any weight. They became listless and started to die. The only difference was contact.

Have you ever seen a shooting star and then quickly look over to tell someone what you saw or see a rainbow and call everyone out from the house to come see it? We want to share these moments with others. It's how we connect to each other that gives meaning to life's experiences. We bond to each other and have a sense of belonging as we live through a common event, similar to graduating from the same school or serving in the military together. Some of the best friends I have, I met going to the same church or living on the same block. My friends and I share a common history. This alone is not what makes us friends, but it is where it started. To build an enduring friendship you have to take the time. Time to have fun and time to do the stuff only your friend will do, help you move or take you to the airport. Most friendships are also built on trust. Sharing your history and secrets, not all at once, but over time, brings you closer to real friendship. I have about five or six very close friends that I can trust. Some I have known for about five years and some for over thirty years. We don't always talk, but if I ever need anything or if they do we are there for each other. Be a loyal friend. Do not take your friendships for granted.

When Christopher Reeves was thrown from a horse and suffered a severe neck injury, he was unable to keep up with all the medical bills that just kept coming. Reeves had a young family to provide for in addition to the cost of all the health problems he had to face. Most people may not know that Christopher Reeves and Robin Williams were very close friends. Robin took over paying all the bills for the Reeves Family. He had to work harder to make enough money to cover all the extra expenses, taking on films sometimes more for the paycheck then for the project itself, and Williams never boasted about his deeds. These friends loved each other in the good times and when it counted most. We should all aspire to share a friendship like this.

"Love is that condition in which the happiness of another person is essential to your own"
Robert A. Heinlein

LAW #6

Don't wait for permission to live. If you feel you need it, I give it to you. There, no more excuses.

"It's better to ask for forgiveness than permission," or so I've heard. I think this saying has come about because so many people are on the sidelines of life waiting for someone, anyone, to tell them its okay to follow their dreams. We are conditioned to follow "*the rules*" doing what we are told to do even when these so called *rules* don't always make sense. For example, it seems the world is telling our young people that they must have a college degree to be successful. But is that really the case? Do you have to have a college degree, and is it always the smartest thing you can do? Well, today over 40% of all college graduates are employed in jobs that do not require a college degree, not to mention all of the kids who have racked up tens of thousands of dollars in student loan debt and didn't even graduate. Think of all the young people in this situation carrying this debt and trying to start their lives. The worst part is that none of this debt can be discharged in bankruptcy. If you had borrowed money to start a business and the business failed that debt could be discharged in a BK, but not student loans, and they give them out like candy. Don't get me wrong, I believe some careers do require college and lots of it. I don't want to see a doctor that hasn't been to medical school, nor would I want to drive across a bridge engineered by a high school dropout.

Let's be honest, rule breakers change the world. They are creative, outside of the box thinkers. They innovate and often times blaze a new trail we all end up following. Look at Bill Gates. He sold IBM an operating system he didn't even own. Steven Spielberg gained access to the sets of Universal Studios by posing as an executive from the east coast office. There he studied directing, watching and learning from the masters up close. He honed his craft and became one of the greats. Colonel Sanders didn't get his start in the restaurant chicken business until he was sixty-five years old. All he had was a recipe of eleven herbs and spices. He had no experience in the food industry, or running any kind of business. It was no wonder Sanders had trouble getting financing for his fledgling restaurant. But none of that would stop him from changing the way the world eats chicken.

Sometimes the best thing you can do is just go for it. Work it out as you go. You will learn as you move forward. The only guarantee in life is that if you aim at nothing you will surely hit it. So get in the game and shoot for the moon. The clock is ticking.

"People are just as happy as they make their minds up to be."
Abraham Lincoln

LAW #7

Never waste a minute bemoaning getting older. 1) You can't change it. 2) It beats the alternative. 3) It is the youngest you will ever be again...Enjoy it!

It is true that from the moment we take our first breath we start the process of dying (how's that for a book on happiness). This is not to be morose, but to heed the warning of time. The clock is uncertain, but what is sure is that we all have a limited amount of time to create the lives we want. This is a great thing, it keeps us from procrastinating. As we get older we gain perspective. We start to be able to distinguish between what is and is not important. We can better prioritize the things that will bring us peace and happiness. It is important to remember that each stage of life has something to offer. So what is old? Is it a certain age? Is seventy old? Would you say that Jack Lalanne was old when he celebrated his seventieth birthday by swimming over a mile through Long Beach Harbor towing seventy boats full of people while his feet and hands were shackled? Does that sound like an old man to you? So maybe swimming a mile towing seventy boats full of your closest friends isn't your thing, but isn't it cool to know it's possible? We are an amazing species. Ordinary people of all ages can and *do* accomplish extraordinary things. Do not let anyone make you feel old no matter how old you become. Life is meant to be enjoyed, not endured. Know that every day is a gift that you can either treasure or waste. So don't waste a minute.

> **"Count your age by friends, not years. Count your life by smiles not tears."**
> **John Lennon**

LAW #8

If you want to be a happier person stop worrying about what others think of you. All people are self-absorbed. No one is spending too much time thinking of you.

Just to let you know, the guys in the huddle aren't talking about you either. Can you believe how self conscious some people are? You've seen them. They are always changing their clothes again and again before leaving the house. Spending more time worrying about what they're going to say next in a conversation rather than listening to what's being said. Always feeling they are going to come up short or not quite measure up somehow. The truth is most people are more concerned with their own problems than passing judgment on you. If you can start caring more about what you think, and less about what anyone else thinks you're on your way. I heard a pastor once say, "when I was in my twenties, I worried about what people thought of me. When I was in my forties, I didn't care what people thought of me. Now that I'm in my sixties, I realized no one was ever thinking of me." He's right. No one wakes up in the morning and says, "I wonder what Bill's doing." I'm just not that important, especially to people I barely know. If you don't try to please the world, and why should you, you have a good chance of being pleased with yourself. Besides, I have found that most of the time we are far more critical of ourselves than the people we try to please.

> **"The most important thing is to enjoy your life-to be happy-it's all that matters."**
> **Audrey Hepburn**

LAW #9

Have standards. They must be *your* standards or they are of little value. Keep and hold yourself to them. They will help you have structure and integrity.

If you stand for nothing you will fall for anything. Today popular culture seems to hold no absolutes. No right, no wrong, no black, no white, just a world of gray. Situational ethics are taught everyday in colleges across this country. Once doing the right thing was a value held by our entire society. Today the elite would have you think that the notion of being principled was an antiquated idea, but I contend that this is a value that is more important than ever. Keeping your word both to others and to yourself is a matter of self respect. Be someone who can be trusted. The next time you are given too much change at the store or bank, give it back. I know it's tempting to keep it, but what would you really get $10, $20, $100. What is your integrity worth? How much can you be bought for? Your integrity should be priceless. When you hold yourself up to a high standard, you feel valuable, especially in a world without values.

Standards help us stay on the right path as we navigate our way through life. They give us a code of conduct to follow. You will deal with people not governed by any such code, but this should not negate your principles as you deal with them. Do what is right to others so you can feel good about how you behave. You'll sleep better, I promise.

> "I am very happy because I have conquered myself and not the world. I am very happy because I have loved the world and not myself."
> Sri Chnmoy

LAW #10

The only thing you can always have control over is your attitude. It can make a bad situation better and a good situation great.

Your attitude is like your emotional thermostat. It can be hot outside and all around you, but you can stay cool. Your attitude is controlled by you, and no one else. How you see the things in your life and what you tell yourself it means, will dictate your attitude. Say you're meeting a friend at Starbucks at 10:00 AM. Your friend stands you up. Your attitude could be, "That jerk just wasted my whole morning," or it could be "I hope my friend is alright," it depends on what you tell yourself it means. Have you ever heard someone say, "They make me so mad,"? It isn't true. You choose to be mad or not to be mad, it's up to you. Don't get me wrong, it's not easy, but it's still a choice.

I had a friend years ago whose name was Angie. She was a very special girl who came from a very special family. When she was nineteen years old, she was heading back to college with her three friends. Angie was sitting in the back of the car when the driver fell asleep. The car rolled and Angie was killed, no one else was hurt. Angie's parents had a memorial service for her that I attended. You see, Angie was raised as a Christian. Her parents believe she is in heaven and that they will see her again. Neither her mother or father cried or even looked sad at the service. Their attitude was governed by what they believed death meant.

Your outlook on the events in your life will directly influence the degree of happiness you will experience. Don't be negative. Your attitude will affect the people around you. When you walk into a room you can either be a fragrance or a stench. It's your choice.

> **"The greater part of our happiness or misery depends on our dispositions and not upon our circumstances."**
> **Martha Washington**

LAW #11
Avoid making your identity your career or your possessions. Instead find your value in your talents, your family, and the way you live your life. For you may lose your job or have your possessions taken, then where will you be?

Why do adults like to pretend that they are more than they really are just because they have a high paying career, live in a big house or drive a nice car? Remember nobody likes the pretentious. Accomplishments are great and should be enjoyed, but what you do is not who you are. Every day jobs are lost in this country and in fact many families have also lost their homes. These are events largely out of our control, but nevertheless, do change our lives. If your self-image is erroneously linked to your station in life and your life takes a turn for the worse, you now have two problems: one financial and the other emotional.

Remember the crash of 1929 and the great depression? When the stock market crashed there were men who lost their entire fortunes. Some of these men could not bear the loss of their money, their position or lifestyle. With no regard to their wives or children these men jumped to their deaths leaving behind no one to look out for their families.

Never put how you feel about yourself into the hands of others, for this is the one thing you need to guard jealously.

"Learn to value yourself, which means: fight for your happiness."
Ayn Rand

LAW #12

Forgiving those who wrong you is the gift you give yourself.

To err is human. To forgive is divine. We all need forgiveness from time to time, but are we good at offering forgiveness to others? So many people think holding on to a grudge is an acceptable way of being. These same people seek forgiveness for their transgressions while denying it to others.

When you refuse to forgive someone who has hurt you, you hold on to that pain and resentment. It has been said that holding this emotional poison can actually make you physically sick.

My friend Dave was cheated on by his ex-wife with their pastor who was counseling them. He was double betrayed and she hurt him very deeply. Even after Dave was divorced he was not ready to forgive her. He started having heart problems and ended up in the hospital. Dave believes that all the hurt and hatred he carried around with him led to his health problems.

As you go through life, people will hurt, cheat, and betray you. Each offense that you don't forgive is like a stone you pick up on your path and place in a large bag you carry with you. Your burden grows heavier with each stone you collect, weighing you down. As you start to forgive these wrongs, you unburden yourself one stone at a time, lightening your load.

The goal is to learn to forgive as fast as possible and to never carry that burden with you. Remember, if there is someone you aren't forgiving, it doesn't hurt them, it only makes you a slave to bitterness. So forgive and live free.

> **"For every minute you are angry you lose sixty seconds of happiness"**
> **Ralph Waldo Emerson**

LAW #13

Never pretend to be what others want you to be. For if you are not free to be who and what you are for fear of disappointing others, you will feel like a fraud and only end up resenting those you have tried to protect.

How can anyone be happy walking someone else's path? Life is short, but not being true to yourself can make it seem like an eternity. Most people struggle to find themselves, to really know who they are. So how much of a waste is it to know who you are and what you want to be, but feel like you have to edit yourself to be accepted? Perhaps you want to sing or dance, but come from a family whose expectations and support are tied to academic achievement. Perhaps their dreams are of you becoming a doctor or an attorney. We have all heard of the stage parent who attempts to live out their dreams of stardom through their son or daughter, only to ruin their child's life in the process. It's almost imperceptible how you can become trapped by the invisible chains of expectations. The secrets people keep, for fear of rejection, are as varied as the people themselves. From education to sexual orientation and from financial to an illicit past are all things people hide. The ironic part is that the ones you feel will judge you generally mean well and are motivated by love, and only want to see you happy. This is the truth you must cling to. When you know something about yourself that you are afraid to voice, something true, remember that this is *your* life. You only get one. All the people in your life that may be critical about your choices were already given a life of their own to run. Don't give them yours. Besides, if they are motivated by love they will learn to respect you and take the time to understand. But if control is their only motivator, then live your truth and buy them a robot.

> **"The secret to happiness is freedom; the secret of freedom is courage."**
> **Carrie Jones Need**

LAW #14
Jealousy is the crystal meth of the soul. It pulls you down into a deep dark hole, and you end up alone.

Being happy is not just about doing the right things to make you happy, but also about identifying and avoiding the things that may cause despair. Jealousy is called the green eyed monster for a reason. There is nothing that can make you feel as angry, desperate, pathetic, worthless and alone as jealousy. These are powerful emotions that can be hard to control. For some, the hurt is so deep, it lights a fire of violent destruction that consumes them and all they hold dear. But for most of us it's just miserable.

I once knew a young lady that worked at a check cashing place, she was about twenty-seven years old, and I used to see her about five time a week. One Monday I went into the store and this young lady wasn't working. I asked Dean, the manager, where she was. Dean told me that she did not come to work and she had not called. He was worried because this was not like her. She was out all week, and on Friday Dean told me he was going to go by her place to drop off her paycheck. On Monday when I came into the store I asked Dean if he had heard from the young woman and what he told me I will never forget as long as I live. Dean said that when he went over to her house it looked as if no one had been there all week, newspapers stacked up, and the mailbox was full. But her car was in the driveway. Dean called the police. They came and opened the door and the smell of death was thick in the air. This poor young lady had been going through a contentious divorce, and had been seeing a new man. She had three small children that she sent to Texas to visit her parents, so thank God they were not home. Her estranged husband came over in a jealous rage and with a large butcher knife he slaughtered his wife and smeared her blood all over the walls. He then killed himself leaving behind three young orphans. His jealousy destroyed everything.

Jealousy can be a self-fulfilling prophecy. You can hold on to the one you love so tightly that you end up choking off any love they have left. It's human nature. The harder you try to hold on to someone, the more they want to be free.

When I was nineteen I was jealous for a long and painful weekend. I felt out of control and it gave me a stomachache. I hated it so much that I came up with a way to stop being jealous, a new way of thinking about jealousy that may also make sense to you.

1. Like yourself and know that you have something to offer, know you are a good

catch. Know how to treat a mate, and make them feel loved and cherished.
2. If the person you love doesn't want to be with you, do you want them to pretend to love you, or to stay with you out of pity? Hell No!
3. Do you really want someone who doesn't want you? Someone who can't see all you have to offer?
4. Trust them, love them, and if they want out, let them go. They're not the right one for you. Don't waste your heart on someone who cannot see what you have to give. So find another, because you deserve to be loved.

Think about it. If they don't love you why would you want them? Really? So if that makes sense to you kiss jealousy goodbye.

> **"Success is getting what you want; happiness is wanting what you get."**
> W.P. Kinsella

LAW #15

Money may not buy you happiness, but the lack of it can ruin your whole day. Do not ignore your finances.

The Bible says that the *love* of money is the root of all evil. Not that money is evil. Money is a tool that may be used for good or bad. The love of money is responsible for theft, deceit, and murder. However, we all need money. You can't get away from it. This is possibly the most important section in this book to escape household stress. Read it carefully. In fact, financial stress is cited as the most common cause of divorce in America. So with that being said, if you learn to manage your finances properly you will be able to avoid one of life's most common problems in society. First you will want to deal with your debt, and the interest that comes with it. Creating a strong financial future and carrying debt is like trying to fill a bucket with holes at the bottom, try as you might, it just won't fill. There are many different kinds of debt, car, house, credit cards. We love to buy with credit. Buy now and pay later. Each loan payment has both principal and interest. Your interest rate will vary with each loan and each kind of loan. Do everything you can to make sure your payments are made on time. Your credit rating has probably the most direct effect on the amount of interest you will pay. The rates on home loans are typically lower than say car loans or credit cards, but they all carry interest which will erode your wallet and keep you a slave to the banks.

Find extra money in your budget to pay down your debt. This is really more fun than it sounds. It could be that $5 morning cup of coffee, or you could eat out less. When you start looking at it, you will be surprised how much money you waste each week. Take as much extra money as you can come up with and apply it each month to the principal of the loan with the smallest balance. As soon as this loan is paid off then start on the loan with the next smallest balance applying both your usual monthly payment and all the extra money that you had been applying to pay off the first loan, and so on and so on. You can use this method to pay off your credit cards, your car and even your house, and it will save you thousands of dollars in interest. When I was thirty-eight years old I had paid off my house, my cars and all my credit cards, I was completely out of debt. It felt great, and you can do the same thing. With each loan you pay off, the amount you will have to apply to your next loan will increase, and you will be out of debt before you know it.

Now that you're on your way to becoming debt free, you need to start the second part of building a sound financial future. This may all seem like dry stuff, but if you give it a chance you will be very happy.

As your debt subsides your cash flow will increase. This will make it easier to take at least 10% of everything you make and set it aside. Don't make the mistake of hoping you have 10% at the end of the month. Take the first 10% of everything that comes in and set it aside before you pay any of your bills. This money will grow very quickly. This money is for you to invest into something that will grow and make you money. The goal is to have your money start making you money. If you start now and repeat this year after year, you will sidestep all money problems that plague the average American.

"Everyone wants to live on top of the mountain, but all the happiness and growth occurs while you're climbing it."
Andy Rooney

LAW #16

Happiness is not a destination, but the journey of a lifetime. It's filled with milestones, triumphs, and challenges. Sometimes the path is crowded. Sometimes we walk alone. Our task is to find beauty even in the struggle.

This truth was illustrated to me back in the early 80's when a friend of mine named Carman was trying to break into the Christian Music business. He had been singing and writing songs for years with some success, but not really breaking through. Carman wanted to get a recording contract so he could finally earn a living with his music. He had been working for a company that reupholstered booths for Denny's Restaurants. One day Carman met a popular Christian singer named Andre Crouch. They hit it off and Andre was instrumental in helping Carman get signed to record his first album. Carman was ecstatic, and so were his friends and family. We were all so proud of him. Carman worked on the songs for that first album day and night. There was so much anticipation for not just that album, but for the start of his whole career. I remember seeing Carman after his album was released. I thought he'd be over the moon with glee, but he actually seemed a little down. He told me that he had wanted this recording contract and this album for so long, that when he got it, it was like, "Is that all there is?" He was grateful to have it, but he thought it would feel more satisfying than it did. Carman was driven to succeed. It never occurred to him that even if he got what he wanted it might not be enough. So he decided that from then on he would be less about the destination and more about savoring the ride along the way. Well, Carman's journey continued, he went on to be a very successful recording artist. He also runs *Carman Ministries* and has his own show on a Christian channel. Some of his recordings include *The Champion*, and *Spirit Filled Pizza*. He has sold over ten million albums. In 1990 Billboard magazine rated Carman the Contemporary Christian Artist of the Year.

We all have a tendency to do what Carman did. We get so caught up looking forward to some end goal or destination that we overlook the journey that took us there. It doesn't occur to us that when we arrive at our destination we may be left feeling empty. The journey is what gives satisfaction to the destination. The goal is anticlimactic without appreciating the journey.

Remember when you were a child and Christmas was the biggest day of the year? You waited for it, you made a list of what you wanted Santa to bring you. You tried really hard to be good, especially the closer it got to Christmas. Maybe your Mom took you to the mall to go see Santa in person, and sit on his lap. Your family would go together to pick out a Christmas tree. You'd all decorate the tree while Christmas music played, and the smell of fresh baked cookies would fill the air. You and your brothers and sisters would search the house to see where your parents hid your presents. Finally it was Christmas morning. You awoke before anyone else in the house and you still had to wait for your Mom and Dad to get up. So you would pester them with your Christmas enthusiasm until they finally arose. Then the moment you waited all year long for is right in front of you, the tree with all the presents around it. Christmas was finally here.

It would take your family about an hour to open up all the presents and you'd play with a couple of new toys for awhile, but by that afternoon you were bored.

When you stop and think about it, the true joy of Christmas is really found in the anticipation and the journey, just as it is with life.

> "Happiness is not a goal…it's a by-product of a life well lived."
> **Eleanor Roosevelt**

LAW #17

Be your own best friend. Accept yourself. Learn from your mistakes, and then forgive yourself. You are no good to others if you keep punishing yourself.

There are things in all of our lives that we regret. Things we are ashamed of and wish we could change. Sometimes it's the hurtful things we say that we can't take back. None of us hold a monopoly on bad decisions. The good news is that we regret them. This means we have grown enough to be able to recognize our past mistakes. It's not unusual for people in your life to hold your past against you. This can make you feel like you don't deserve to be forgiven, and subconsciously you may do things to punish yourself. If this is your mind set, you will have trouble accomplishing your goals or finding any real happiness. You can't live like that.

When I was young I spent a lot of time alone. I had friends, but still there were times when I preferred my own company. I thought kids were cruel and cliquish. I learned to be my own best friend. This meant I had to start to like myself. When I did something I would regret, or I made a mistake, I would attempt to make it right if I could. Then I would try to learn from my mistakes, forgive myself, and move on. You have to be your own best friend in this life. If you are not on your own side, who will be? It would be like running for office and instead of voting for yourself, you vote for the other guy. So many people think that if they don't forgive themselves that it's somehow noble, or to be commended. It's not. You can't afford it. You can't afford the time, the energy, or the distraction. If you have asked God for forgiveness He will give it to you. So if God forgives you, how can you not forgive yourself? Are your standards higher than God's? The truth is we are all flawed human beings, and everyone screws up. But we grow and we learn and we change. If you didn't believe that, you would not be reading this book. So let go of your regrets, and know that your past doesn't have to equal your future. Give yourself a break so you can focus on becoming the best version of you possible. Then maybe you will have something to give to those around you that need you.

"Until you make peace with who you are, you'll never be content with what you have."
Doris Mortman

LAW #18

It's sharper than any two edged sword. It can bring comfort, encouragement and wisdom. With the next breath it can dispense lies, hatred and malice, but if you can tame your tongue, you can prevent regret.

"Sticks and stones..." we have heard it before, but it's just another popular lie. The truth is, if the sticks and stones don't kill you, you will heal in a couple of weeks. The words used to tease and torment kids can stay with them for a lifetime. Just ask anyone who was mercilessly made fun of as a child.

Words can also incite riots and even start wars. Think of the last time your whole family got together. All it took was a careless word to a sensitive family member, then there was yelling and hurt feelings and the whole day was ruined. Or maybe that's just my family.

I like to joke around and have fun, but sometimes my jokes may hit a nerve and I end up causing pain to someone I never intended to hurt. This is the power of a quick and reckless tongue. If we can hurt each other unintentionally, how much more devastation do the words spoken in anger or with a callous disregard cause?

Be trustworthy. Gossip and rumors can tear apart even the best friendships. When you share a secret with someone, you are opening yourself up to possibly being hurt and betrayed. Being vulnerable in the world can be a scary thing for most of us, so be careful who you confide in.

The tongue can bring healing just as it can spark the fires of destruction. Speaking gentle words of reason to guide and give perspective to someone in need can bring both comfort and understanding in order to build and sustain a friendship.

Give every effort to bridle your tongue. Speak your mind prudently. Avoid rash personal attacks. You will have less to apologize for and you may be able to avoid causing pain that can last a lifetime. Whenever possible encourage those around you. They may need it and you will find yourself a happier person for doing so.

"Happiness is a gift and the trick is not to expect it, but to delight in it when it comes."
Charles Dickens

LAW #19

Put your mind on a diet. Stay away from the evening news. Avoid stories of tragic events. Instead dwell on all things that are good and uplifting.

We all know the world is full of heart breaking events. Earthquakes, hurricanes, murders and high taxes are in the news just about every day, but you don't need to ingest all this negativity right before you go to bed. Sweet dreams? Good luck!

That being said, I don't want you to live with your head in the sand either. Set aside a day or two to wade into all the messy news and current events. This way you are not ignorant of the world around you and you are slowing the tide of depressing news that left unchecked can swallow you up.

There are so many good stories of courage and sacrifice you can find that can challenge and encourage you to make a difference in the world around you. We tend to reflect what we dwell on. If you dwell on crime stories, then you may feel afraid, where if you dwell on the triumph of the human spirit you may find yourself inspired.

"Remember, happiness doesn't depend upon who you are or what you have, it depends solely upon what you think."
Dale Carnegie

LAW #20

Hope is the ship that carries the soul. It is impossible to be happy without it.

Hope is more than a wish. It is the possibility of something longed for. It can even affect the outcome of events. I remember years ago hearing about a study where they took a mouse and put it in a bucket of water to see how long it could swim before it would drown. The first mouse swam for about 13 minutes before it got tired and drowned. The second mouse swam for about 12 minutes before it too got tired and drowned. The third mouse was put in the water and it swam for about 13 minutes before it also got tired and started to drown, but this time they pulled the mouse out of the water and saved this one. They dried it off, fed it and let it rest 10 hours. Then they put this same mouse back into the bucket of water a second time to see how long it could swim. While the average time had been only about 13 minutes per mouse, this time the mouse swam for 22 minutes before it started to falter. The 9 minute difference was hope. The mouse had the hope that if it could just hang in there a little while longer it would be rescued once again. Once again it would be dried off, and once more it would be fed. The outcome was changed because of hope. We hear of people stranded in the wilderness, or plane crash victims lasting without food or shelter much longer than anyone would have thought possible. When asked how they survived so long out in the elements, or how they kept going, they would say they just kept hoping someone would find them. We have all heard the saying, "keep hope alive," but it can also be said, hope keeps us alive. Hope can sustain us even in the face of an uncertain future. Hope is one of the cornerstones of most religions, knowing we have a place to go to when we pass from this life, hoping that some supreme justice will balance the scales in the end and set all things right. This can also give us hope that in the here and now someone cares and sees our struggles and has a plan we may not be able to see. I would not want to live in a world without hope, nor would anyone else.

I love the line in the movie *Cast Away*, "You never know what the tide's going to bring in." Each day brings new hope and opportunities for each of us. If you truly want to be happy find reasons for hope. Guard it. And look forward to tomorrow.

> **"Hope smiles from the threshold of the year to come, whispering "it will be happier"…"**
> **Alfred Tennyson**

LAW #21

Music can restore the soul and bring joy to the heart, but be careful of all things nostalgic. It can be bitter sweet, yet spark the flames of depression and a yearning for yesterday.

We all should hold a song in our hearts. The Bible says King David encouraged himself in the Lord with music when the enemy came and attacked his camp. Music has been used to bring joy in every culture known to man. We hum, we sing, we dance. Music can lift us up when we are down, and touch us in a deeply personal way. We sing songs of worship and songs of love, and let's face it, it just makes us happy. We listen to our favorite music as we work, drive, and play. Music can take us back in time to an exact moment in our life. We can remember where we were, and who we were with and what we were doing. We can see every detail and feel all the emotions of that time in our life. This can be comforting in small doses, but be careful you don't start to idealize your past. Sometimes when we are going through a rough patch in our life, we are all too vulnerable to a kind of nostalgic poison. Wistfully telling ourselves it was better long ago, or it will never be like it was. Looking back is only helpful to gain perspective on one's life, not in the longing to relive it. A joyful optimism is found as we let go of the past and we look forward to the future. We can bring great music from our past into today and avoid the pitfalls of depression by incorporating it into our present day activities and creating new memories that will link to our favorite old songs.

Music can also inspire and create a cohesive bond uniting a group or even a country. Think of the songs used to unite a college at a football game, or national anthem used to inspire a people to think and act as one. Movies use music to help tell a story and let us know how to feel about an event or a character. Think about how you feel watching Rocky training for the big fight. The music swells and you feel like getting in the ring yourself. We can use the way music makes us feel to help motivate us to work out, face challenges, and to overcome the odds. So lift your heart, and sing it loud.

"A happy heart makes its own song."
Barbara Jean

LAW #22

If laughter is the best medicine, then take two jokes and call me in the morning.

Life goes better with a good sense of humor. Finding something funny, even in tense situations is a very valuable skill. Learning to laugh at ourselves is a great first step in being able to maintain mental health. Don't be a sourpuss. A hundred years from now whatever you're dealing with won't seem so bad. (Not even to you) On the day President Reagan was shot he was quoted as telling his wife, "I forgot to duck." He knew how to find humor even in the darkest moments of life. My favorite Reagan quote goes like this, "The nine most dangerous words are, I'm with the government, and I'm here to help." People who don't laugh may not live longer but it will just feel like life is taking forever. The truth is, laughter really is the best medicine. It releases a hormone that helps our immune system, and it helps relieve stress. People need to laugh. This is why sitcoms like *Seinfeld* and *Friends* have been so successful over the years. Ever since there has been entertainment there has been comedy. Find what makes you laugh and enjoy it. It may be a movie or a TV show or a stand-up comic. Share something funny with your friends and family. Life is short and should be enjoyed not endured. So enjoy laughing with your friends and family and don't be afraid of looking foolish as you spread your own unique brand of humor with a world in need of cheer.

> "If more of us valued food and cheer and song above hoarded gold, it would be a merrier world."
> **J.R.R. Tolkien**

LAW #23

Avoid needless confrontation over small matters with petty people.

We are all different people with backgrounds as varied as the sands of the sea. It's no wonder sometimes we just don't click with everyone we meet. Some people are kind and treat others with respect, while some may be a little harder to be around. We don't know what in a person's life has come before that moment we encounter them. A person's past may play into how they react in any situation. For this reason, never assume other people will behave as you expect them to. A small conflict with the wrong person can be transformed into a life threatening confrontation. We have all heard of people being killed over something trivial. Even if no one's getting hurt, a person who has a hair trigger temper may make our life miserable if they feel we've crossed them. This is not to say that we need to be doormats, or that we can't stand up for ourselves, but don't major on the minors. Fighting over something just so you can be right, or standing on some principle merely to make a point can be destructive as well as petty. We've all heard, "don't sweat the small stuff," the trick is distinguishing between what is and isn't small. When you can do that, you can learn to let go and let them win. It's not worth it. Move on to the important things in your life. You only have so much energy to go around.

Avoid "jackasses". These are the people in your life that cause you so much frustration you start talking to yourself. Wish them no harm and get away from them. Nothing good will come from your association with aggravating people. Let jackasses deal with other jackasses.

> **"The best way to cheer yourself is to try to cheer someone else up."**
> **Mark Twain**

LAW #24
Indecision is the enemy of happiness. Make a decision, and be happy.

Fish or cut bait, crap or get off the pot, don't change horses in mid stream; you can't have your cake and eat it too. These all describe how the world feels about indecision. No one has ever been applauded for their inability to make a decision. We call it waffling when a Politician seeks to have both sides of an issue. Don't waffle. Hard decisions are unavoidable. Ducking tough choices is a sure path to falling short of a happy life. Being "*torn*" between two ideas even sounds painful. Most of the time when we don't make a decision it is due to our fear of making a mistake. This worry over being wrong can be paralyzing for people who either want to avoid embarrassment or simply need to be right. The truth is, sometimes we just won't know the right decision to make, and that's okay. If we make the best decision we can with the information we have, we don't need to second guess ourselves. If the decision we make is wrong we will find out soon enough. At that point, if need be, we can make a new decision. This is not an argument for being hasty, but being stuck in the in between or left up in the air leaves no room for peace. In life we have all sorts of choices we must make. If we become a doctor, we cannot be a baseball player. If we travel north we can't go south. If we put off making a decision this becomes a decision in and of itself.

Several years ago I let an employee of mine live in my garage. He had a severe alcohol problem that was getting worse. He would be so drunk he couldn't even speak. He could only cry as I put a blanket over him. I wanted him to get into treatment but he didn't want to go. So I put it off because I didn't want to make him feel any worse than he already did. This went on for a year. I didn't want this responsibility, I wanted him to make his own decision, but he was addicted. He was not able to make good decisions on his own. I realized the only loving thing I could do was to find him a bed at a treatment center and tell him he could either, get in the car and let me take him to treatment or he could move on, but he could not spend another night in my garage. My employee got the help he needed and his whole life changed. Today he is a clean, sober, successful and happy man.

Practice making small decisions and the big ones will come easier. If you can learn to be decisive, you can learn to lead.

"Action may not always bring happiness, but there is no happiness without action."
William James

LAW #25

You can't please everyone. Set boundaries and learn the word "No."

We all want to be liked, appreciated and needed. This is how we get sucked into doing too much for too many. It starts out small, being asked for a little favor. Next thing we know we're in over our head and the weight of expectation is crushing. We don't have time to do what we are asked and everything's important. We are so afraid of letting someone down that we put all our own needs on the back burner. Soon we start to resent those we are trying to help. Worst of all we have said "yes" to way too many people and become so overcommitted that we don't have the time to do what we promised. Enough!

This was me years ago, when someone told me I needed to learn the word, "no." This person brought a very important point to my attention. I was being unfair by agreeing to do too much at once. If I had said, "No I don't have time," it would have given them the opportunity to find someone who *did* have the time and ability to help them, instead of trusting someone who really had no business agreeing to one more commitment.

Be wise. Decide what's important in your life and give yourself enough time to accomplish your goals and priorities. Help when you can, but do not over commit, and learn how to say, "No."

> "Very little is needed to make a happy life; it is all within yourself in your way of thinking."
> Marcus Aurelius

LAW #26

You can't make a good deal with a bad person.

Look, we all want to be happy, right? The best way to screw it up is by getting involved with a bad person. If you know the person is unscrupulous or has been dishonest with someone else, stay away. Bad people only care about themselves. Don't fool yourself by thinking they only treat *other* people bad or unfair, but not you. It's only a matter of time. Often, when we get caught up with a bad guy, it is due to our own greed. Deep inside we know better, but the promise of financial gain can sometimes cloud our judgment. If we make a deal with a bad person and that person does something illegal, we may be held responsible. That would suck. Ending up in a jail cell might not be in your plan for a happier life.

How many people trusted Bernie Madoff and lost everything? Sometimes you may not know you're dealing with the devil and you will get deceived. When you know the person across the table has questionable ethics you only have one logical course of action you can take. Run. Run as fast as you can.

I did a real estate deal once with a bad guy and I lost tens of thousands of dollars and ended up being sued for the actions of said bad guy. It was a nightmare and I learned my lesson.

> "There is only one way to happiness and that is to cease worrying about things which are beyond the power of our will."
> Epictetus

LAW #27

Whistle while you work, but work. It gives meaning to life and a reason to get out of bed.

Work, for too many people, is just another four letter word, something to be avoided, or to get out of the way. We dream about winning the lottery so we can quit our jobs and sleep in. Would this make us happy? Maybe for a little while, but soon the novelty of all this free time would turn into boredom and lose its appeal. What about the rich? Donald Trump or Warren Buffet, these men have more money than they can spend, yet each still works. If it's not a need for money that drives them, then it's because the work gives them something apart from the money, a purpose.

Work connects us to our community and gives us a way to contribute to the world around us. When a man loses his job and he is used to working, he tends to feel lost. The price of too much free time is an erosion of spirit. We see it in the eyes of the homeless, a forgotten usefulness of days long gone. Work gives us a sense of self respect and the respect of others. Mankind needs to work. It keeps us out of trouble. (Idle hands...) It allows us to create and gives us an opportunity to become social. When this is taken away from us the change can take its toll. When a person is forced to retire after a lifetime of employment, not only can it affect them financially but can be emotionally devastating and undermine their sense of value.   We forget that work is a privilege. When we see the number of unemployed across this country, we are reminded of how lucky we are when we have the chance to work.

I think Garth Brooks said it best. When he first came out of retirement, he said he wouldn't wish retirement on his worst enemy.

> "They say a person needs just three things to be truly happy in this world: someone to love, something to do, and something to hope for."
> Tom Bodett

LAW #28

Sometimes the members of our family have tails.   Pets are little furry bundles of unconditional love. They need us and we need them.

Millions of pets all across the globe fill a need for love and companionship. From the time we are children we learn how to make room in our hearts for our pets. Dogs, cats, lizards, birds and fish have all become family members to those who love them. Having a loving pet that depends on us gives us a reason to care about something other than ourselves. Our pets are also great listeners. We can be ourselves with them in a way we can't with almost anyone else. They don't judge us. Some prisons are now using cats to help socialize inmates and give them something to care about.

The death of a pet can be heartbreaking, and for most of us it was the first time as children we had ever dealt with death. The grief we feel for the loss of a pet directly corresponds with the happiness they brought us.

My oldest son suffers from a sometimes debilitating form of OCD He would go weeks and sometimes months not being able to function in the world outside of our home. He spent days and nights on the sofa in our living room trapped within his mind full of cycling thoughts he couldn't control. Even though he was surrounded by his family, he was still alone. The only thing that would give him comfort was our cat, Shadow. Shadow would sit on my son's chest keeping him company hour after hour as my son would stroke Shadow's black, fluffy fur. This cat was my sons' constant companion and his only true comfort. Today my son is much better, and though he still has OCD, it is not as all consuming as it once was. Shadow passsed away last year and is sorely missed by the whole family. He was a great cat.

> "Happiness is a warm puppy."
> **Charles M. Schultz**

LAW #29
In life you get what you are willing to settle for.

We all know someone who is married to or dating a person that treats them poorly or with a lack of respect. We ask ourselves, "why?" Why do so many people let themselves be discounted? There are those who work for an abusive boss day after day and wonder why they're unhappy. Hello! It's not healthy to allow anyone to treat you with disrespect. If you don't stand up for yourself, who will? Don't be afraid. People treat you the way you let them. If you require a certain level of respect, you will get it or you won't deal with them.

When young girls give themselves to guys to keep them around, because they feel they have to, this only lowers the value of the girl in the eyes of the guy, and ultimately dooms any chance of a real relationship that is not merely a booty call. Some women date a married man in the hopes he will leave his wife and family. She sits by the phone and waits for his call, living as if she doesn't deserve a man of her own. No man is worth degrading yourself for. I knew a man who was afraid of his wife. He couldn't come over to my house for a half hour without fearing being yelled at. He couldn't spend $5 for lunch. She changed the passwords on his bank accounts. Crazy stuff, I don't get it.

The truth is, if you are willing to settle for the crumbs of disrespect, or a safe level of misery, then no one will stop you. It's your life. But if you want the life you imagined, the life you deserve, the one that will fill your heart with pride, then that too is in your hands. Don't settle for an unhappy life.

"The worst part of success is trying to find someone who is happy for you."
Bette Midler

LAW #30

Never stop learning. It will expand your mind and your opportunities.

As children we learn new things every day, and we suck up information like a sponge. We are curious about the world around us and life is full of wonder. When we start to get older learning new things become more of an inconvenience. I heard a friend of mine say, "I don't want to get a new cell phone; I just learned how to use this one." It is true that learning new things can be frustrating, but it's worth it. Taking time to learn new skills may provide you with a number of benefits.

1. It helps keep your mind young. The exercising of your brain with puzzles and introducing new information to it creates new neurological pathways.

2. It will give you something new and fresh to talk about.

3. Learning new things will keep you relevant. You will participate in the world around you.

4. The more you know, the more opportunities you will have. We are paid in proportion to the value we bring to any task. If you know more, you will

bring more value, and you will take home more money.

I went back to college when I was thirty-eight years old. I had a blast. I loved learning new things every day. It was a lot of work but it was also exciting. The truth is you don't have to go back to school to learn. There is more information on the internet than can be found in one hundred college libraries.

There are clubs you can join having to do with just about any topic under the sun. It can be a great place to learn and meet new friends with common interests. Learning can be easy and fun.

Think of learning a little something every day as a daily vitamin for the brain. Remember that a healthy brain is a happy brain.

"I must learn to be content with being happier than I deserve."
Jane Austen

LAW #31
True, lifelong happiness will only find you when you find your life's calling.

You don't need to hear a voice coming from a burning bush in order to find your calling. A calling can be found in the midst of a tragedy, or in an awakening to an injustice. It can be as large as Gandhi driving out the British from India, or as personal as raising great kids. Your calling is your purpose, your reason for being. It's what fuels your passion day by day. It is the cause that you wake up thinking about each morning and the thing you go to bed each night dreaming about. It doesn't have to make you a penny, or it can be the career you love, but either way it makes you happy.

One of my passions is real estate. I love buying it, selling it, teaching it. I really enjoy helping people learn how to buy homes with little cash or next to no credit. I can talk a person's ear off about real estate, and I have many times, while my poor wife stands by waiting, as I go on and on. I think teaching people how to use real estate to reach their financial goals is my calling. I can't get enough.

In 2002 I met a guy named Tom. I noticed he was working on a NOD list (Notice of Default). I could see he really didn't know what he was doing. So I gave him some pointers. By this time I had flipped dozens of homes. He thanked me and I was on my way. Later that night Tom called me to thank me again and tell me how much he learned in the twenty minutes I spent with him. He also wanted to know how much I would charge to teach him what I knew. I was really surprised. We discussed it and I told him it would be $2000 to take a day and teach Tom and his wife, Michelle as much as I could in a day. They agreed and I took a whole Saturday to fill their heads full with as much knowledge as possible. That was my first real estate student. Over the next ninety days Tom called me about twenty-five times, asking me questions about a deal he was working on, but in the end Tom completed his first real estate deal and made over $90,000 profit. I was so proud. I thought I must be a pretty good teacher. I want to do it again. This is how I got started teaching real estate. So call it a calling, a passion or a cause, it just has to inspire you. When you find the thing that moves you, your happiness will find you.

> "Happiness doesn't result from what we get, but from what we give."
> Ben Carson

LAW #32

It's hard to be happy when you're flabby and out of shape. Don't neglect your health or your body. If you have no energy, and you don't like the way you look, then exercise a little each day.

If you're like me, you hate the thought of exercise. You dread the idea of going to the gym, so you procrastinate. For me, the hardest part about exercising is getting started. That being said, there is nothing you can do for yourself that will give you as many benefits as exercising regularly. We all want to look fit and have more energy, but still we find reasons to put off taking that first step. I say we start today. Don't think about it, just start. Walk around the block. Do a push up, or a leg lift, or ten. Just get started. The more you do the more you'll want to do. Like many men my age I had really declined since my high school water polo days. Once I was hard and fit, but slowly over the years I became soft and fat. I learned that if I wanted to like what I saw in the mirror I and only I had to do something. Here are just a few reasons why I started to work out again: to increase endurance, feel better, relieve stress, have a strong mind and body, to have more energy, create endorphins, look better in clothes, stay younger, keep up with the kids, look more like the guy my wife fell in love with, and can lay out at the beach without Green Peace trying to roll me back into the water, and won't have to Photo-Shop myself out of the family photos.

Look, our bodies have to last a lifetime. We have no problem taking care of our cars. We change the oil every 3,000 miles and inflate the tires. We have to take care of ourselves for us, and for our families. If we don't, who will? There are so many illnesses that can be avoided by how we live and what we eat and yes, if we exercise daily. Living a fit life is one of the few things that only we can control. Take that time every day for yourself. It's okay to be selfish and do what it takes to create a healthier you. Exercise is something you can't save up, it is the daily price we pay to look and feel great. If you work out a little each day it will make you a happier person. I promise.

"Happiness is a state of activity."
Aristotle

LAW #33

The main ingredient in the recipe of a happy life is balance.

All or nothing...we know that too much of even a good thing is bad. There are people who pursue one thing to the exclusion of everything else. This single minded determination may yield great success in this one specific arena, but the lack of attention to anything else in your life can leave you unfulfilled. Even in nature, balance is found between plants and animals. Animals breathe in oxygen and exhale carbon dioxide; plants need our carbon dioxide to give off oxygen, a perfect balance.

There are parents who are so strict and rough it borders on abuse, but at the same time other parents are more concerned with being their kid's friend and give no guidance whatsoever. Balance is *everything* in life.

Workaholics lose their families and the lazy lose their homes. Too serious... they think you're no fun. Always joking... no one takes you seriously. Without balance happiness is illusive.

The topics we've covered in the pages of this book must be taken in balance. Context is just as important as subject in the pursuit of balance and happiness. We should aspire for balance even in our beliefs. Passion for a cause or belief can give life meaning and focus our energy. Extreme positions may gain a lot of attention, but truth is most often found somewhere in the middle.

I can't stress enough; the power of balance will bring peace and happiness in your life. It's worth the effort.

"Human happiness and moral duty are inseparably connected."
George Washington

LAW #34
No man succeeds alone and pride comes before a fall. Do not be afraid to ask for help

Why are we so ashamed to admit we need help? People often fail in life due to a misplaced sense of pride. They fear that they're not good enough or believe that if they don't make it on their own it doesn't count. It would be foolish and shameful if you were not to avail yourself of all resources. Squandering the opportunities around you and neglecting the help others are willing to offer is unwise as well as wasteful. We all need help from time to time to make our dreams come true or to sometimes just survive.

In 1986 I moved my wife and our one year old baby boy from our home in Orange County, California to San Diego to start a Chem-Dry Carpet Cleaning Company. I bought a franchise from Chem-Dry and the only area available was in San Diego. Flash forward a year and a half.

We were in our third apartment, each time moving into a cheaper and cheaper place trying to cover the rent. My wife was pregnant with our second child and we had no insurance and no prenatal care. I had two houses, the one we moved from in Orange County and a small rental we had in Long Beach, both were in foreclosure. I was overdrawn in my bank account and my work van was about to be repossessed. My phone lines were days from being turned off and the rent on our apartment was due the next day. My son Josh, who was two and a half years old by then, had infected flea bites up and down both legs and I had no money to take him to the doctors. I had pawned everything of value by this time and had nothing else to sell, and I had no carpet cleaning jobs booked. We were eating noodles topped with ketchup that I would get from the *Jack in the Box* around the corner. I raided my son's piggy bank and looked under every cushion and in every crack I could to find money to buy diapers and some groceries. I came up with $8.25 to shop for my family's needs and that was literally all I had to my name. I tried to get food stamps but because I owned a house (that was in foreclosure) I didn't qualify and was turned down. I went to the grocery store and filled my basket with diapers, hamburger meat, lettuce and some milk. I stood behind a lady who had two big carts full of groceries and she paid for them all with food stamps. I was envious. My bill came to $8.24 and for the first time in my life I was down to my very last penny. There I was, twenty-four years old with a family I couldn't support and failing in my business. But then I had a moment of clarity. I decided right there in that store parking lot that I would do whatever it took to never let myself or my family be in this position again. I couldn't ask my parents for help as they had passed away a few years earlier, and the only family I had around was my wife's parents. Nobody wants to ask their father-in-law for help.

To make an already long story short, I humbled myself and asked for help. I called my customers from the past year and told them the truth. I told them I was in trouble and offered to clean as much carpet as they wanted for whatever they were willing to pay. I called the customers that were closest to me first because my van was on fumes and I was afraid of running out of gas. They were great. "Sure, Bill we could use a couple of rooms cleaned, come on over," that was how it went one after another. I learned how to negotiate with my creditors and asked them for more time to pay. Yes, I also asked my father-in-law for a loan to save my two properties. (I am against borrowing money unless it's an emergency.) Fortunately I was able to pay him back in 90 days and a few years later I had the privilege of helping my father-in-law when he was in need.

Tell the truth and let people help you. It will give them a chance to make a difference in your life and allow you to show some appreciation. Everyone wins.

"Surely everyone realizes, at some point along the way, that he is capable of living a far better life than the one he has chosen." Henry Miller

LAW #35
The golden nuggets of life are not yielded to the lazy. Be persistent.

If you want to be good at something, you have to be willing to be bad at it first. Some things you want in life are hard to achieve and don't come right away. I teach people how to invest in real estate with both traditional and creative methods. The single most difficult thing to teach someone is persistence.

There once was an experiment using a small cork from a bottle and a 55 gallon drum. Both were suspended by a line from above. The drum hangs there motionless and the cork is tied to a thin silk strand. The cork is swung into the drum over and over in a rhythmic pattern. For a long time it seemingly has no effect on the drum, but after countless impacts with the cork, the drum starts to slowly begin to swing. After many hours the 55 gallon drum is swinging in a wide rhythmic pattern. All from the persistence of a cork weighing about 4 grams.

10% inspiration and 90% perspiration was what Thomas Edison said was the key to success. Greatness is not easily grasped but must be pursued with a dogged determination. When things are easy they are not valued, but the things that take work, time and knowledge are that which we prize most. These are the accomplishments that make us proud and bring us happiness.

I believe that what one man can do, another man can learn to do, with a few exceptions. The truth is, some will learn quickly and some will learn more slowly, but most things can be mastered if there is a desire and determination to do so.

My favorite president is Lincoln. He lost eight elections, failed twice in business, suffered a nervous breakdown, yet still went on to shape a nation. Lincoln was the cork. Be the cork.

"We have no more right to consume happiness without producing it than to consume wealth without producing it."
George Bernard Shaw

LAW #36

Two are better than one. Finding someone to love may be life's true treasure hunt.

Most of us want to share our life with another person. To love and to be loved is a basic desire we all have. Most of us would consider finding a mate to be one of the key elements to a happy life. Don't be afraid to commit to someone you love, or you risk making that person feel alone in the relationship and losing them altogether.

If you want to plan a good first date, take her to do something that will raise her heartbeat, like a roller coaster or a ride on a motorcycle. The goal is to have her anchor the excitement of the event to her thoughts of you, so when she thinks of you she will feel that excitement.

Men and women fall in love in different ways. While dating or when men and women spend time together the woman starts to fall in love with the man during the time she is with him, but a man falls for a woman in the in-between times when he is not with her. The woman responds to the attention that is paid to her. The man idealizes the woman as he misses her and wants to make her his. This dynamic is illustrated most dramatically during a time of war with the "Dear, John" letter. While the boyfriend or husband is off to war, his lady is back at home, all alone. While he is using the thought of his beautiful, loving woman to get him back home, she is left alone in need of attention. All too often she finds that attention from a new suitor, thus, the "Dear, John" letter. The lesson to be learned here is to never leave your woman alone for too long if there's any way to avoid it, and always remember she needs your love and attention.

Love drives the world, so buckle up and take the ride.

> **"Only the development of compassion and understanding for others can bring us the tranquility and happiness we all seek."**
> **Dalai Lama XIV**

LAW #37

Like rain clouds on a summer's day, so disappointment can cast the darkest shadow on an otherwise happy life.

Disappointments are the speed bumps of life. I think there are two types of disappointments we all have to face from time to time. Type one is when you are hoping for something that you really want and it doesn't come to pass for some reason or another. This can take the wind out of your sails for a bit, but is not likely to derail your life or steal your joy for any sustained amount of time. This is because you may want something very badly, but you know there is a real possibility that you may be denied. This prepares you and gives you a shorter recovery time to process that disappointment. Type two is much more dangerous. This is the kind of disappointment that you don't see coming. For instance you find out your wife is cheating on you, or you come into work one day only to be let go. Disappointments that take you by surprise are the kind that does the most damage. It's like the prize fighter who gets hit over and over, and keeps coming, until he is blindsided by that uppercut that lays him flat. When you think that your life is one way, and suddenly you realize your place in this world is not what you thought it was, disappointment is an understatement. These often times are crossroads in a person's life. When you can choose to be defined by that disappointment or to become transformed by the lessons learned and the perspective gained by your unique trials and life experiences. We all have the chance to move past our disappointment and create the happiness we deserve if we can only recognize all the opportunities around us.

The ability to deal with life's disappointments has a direct correlation to our emotional maturity. We have all been around those people who overreact to the smallest problems or can find any reason to become discouraged in their pursuit of happiness. They may be new to hardship or have been overly sheltered, but in either case they could benefit from the perspective that going through troubles can give.

We often find among the residue of our disappointment the seeds of our greatest triumphs. Take Dr. Spencer Silver, a chemist at 3M Company. In 1968 he was working on a new adhesive, a super strong adhesive, but he came up short. He had created a rather weak adhesive instead. At the time he was disappointed because it was good for nothing. No one at 3M could come up with a use for it. Until in 1974 Art Fry, a colleague of Dr. Silver, became frustrated while singing in his church choir because the bookmark in his hymnal kept falling out. He then remembered Silvers' low stick adhesive. He put some on his bookmark and it worked like a charm. The rest was history, Post-It Notes were born.

The seeds of greatness amongst disappointment are not just for the inventor. Take a look at a few disappointing failures.

1. Fired from a newspaper because he had "no imagination and no original ideas." (Walt Disney)
2. Told by a music teacher, "As a composer he is hopeless." (Beethoven)
3. Told by a teacher, he was "too stupid to learn anything." (Thomas Edison)
4. Failed the sixth grade. (Winston Churchill)
5. Wasn't able to speak until he was almost four years old and his teacher said he would "never amount to much." (Albert Einstein)
6. A producer told her she was "too unattractive and couldn't act." (Marilyn Monroe)
7. Cut from his high school basketball team, he went home, locked himself in his room and cried. (Michael Jordan)
8. Received 30 rejections and the author threw it in the trash. Fortunately, his wife fished it out and encouraged him to resubmit it. (The book was Carrie-the author Stephen King)

These are names we all know. We know them because each turned their disappointment into their own brand of success. All great achievements come with their share of failures. Never surrender your hopes, dreams or your joy to the thief that is disappointment.

> **"What great thing would you attempt if you knew you could not fail?"**
> **Dr. Robert H. Shuller**

LAW #38

Teach what you know, share what you love. By passing your knowledge on to the eager, you will help shape the world around you.

Everyone has something they know more about than the average person. In fact, you may be an expert in a field that you are passionate about. There are those who want, and need to know what you know. Sharing your knowledge, skill and interest with someone else can reignite your own passion and create a sense of real satisfaction.

In the 1980's I was a youth minister. I taught junior high and high school kids. I was lucky enough to truly get to know some great kids and their families as I ran the youth program at Sonlight Christian Center in Orange, California. Teaching was something I loved, and still do today. It gave me a sense of purpose, knowing I was impacting young lives and sharing my love of God with them and their families. I have had the privilege of watching some of "my kids" grow up and became doctors, mothers, and an elephant trainer for Michael Jackson's Never Land Ranch for a time. They are all around great people. I still have contact with many of my past youth group students today.

I still enjoy teaching. I hold workshops and do coaching for those who want to learn how to deal with debt and how to buy and sell real estate for profit. My time spent with students helping them achieve their goals has created ripples of influence far beyond my life and has the ability to affect those I will never meet. This can and should encourage you to help mold the minds of the young and anyone who will follow.

So teach what you know and impact the world one student at a time. It's awesome.

> **"Some cause happiness wherever they go; others whenever they go."**
> **Oscar Wilde (1854-1900)**

LAW #39

Put your stamp on the world. Create and be creative. You are one of a kind, and only you can express your unique style. Be proud of what you create and see if it doesn't make you a happier person.

There is a desire to be creative in each of us. We see it all around us. When you think of it, everything we use, read or watch has been created by someone. Although we all have the ability to be creative in some form; many of us suppress our creative impulse because we doubt ourselves. We think that somehow what we create will be judged insufficient and thus criticized. When we suppress our creative juices for fear of what others may think, we are denying a portion of our purpose. Your voice and unique view are just as valuable as anyone else's. The truth is, the more you do the better you will become, and the less you will be worried about anybody else's opinion. Practice your talent and create. You first have to be willing to be bad at something in order to become good at it. That being said, it doesn't matter if everyone thinks your creation, whatever it may be, is great or not so great. The only thing that matters is, do you like your work? Create for your own enjoyment first, and you'll never have to edit yourself.

Creating something that you've poured yourself into is like giving birth. It is a part of you. It makes you proud, and you will show it off to anyone who will let you. I must have read parts of this book to my friends and my poor family over and over again while I was writing it. They were all very gracious and pretended to be interested even in the third and fourth rewrite. The fact is nobody will care about your work the way you do, and that's okay. They don't have to. It's your baby, not theirs.

Vincent Van Gogh was not appreciated for his art while he lived. His work was considered too dark. He had only sold one piece before his death. Today he is thought to be one of the greatest painters of all time. Sadly, he lost his way and took his own life, but he was not afraid to create what he felt.

So do what you do, make what you make, don't worry about the world and just create.

"The best feeling in the world is realizing that you're perfectly happy without the thing you thought you needed."
Marxie

LAW #40

The only thing worse than lending money to friends and family is to borrow from them. Never, ever loan or borrow money when it comes to your friends and family. (Unless it's an emergency.)

It is truly a dangerous road we walk when we consider borrowing or lending from the people we love. More relationships have been ruined by well meaning friends and family that innocently lent or borrowed money. Sadly, it's like Russian roulette for a relationship. The bible says a "borrower is slave to the lender." This is not just a saying, it's a truth.

I said in law #34 that I borrowed money from my father-in-law to save my two properties. It was my very last resort and even though it worked out I was putting that relationship at risk as you do when ever you borrow money from friends or family.

Take the loving mother and father who lent their son and daughter-in-law $30,000 for a down payment on their first home. All is well at first, but as long as the debt is outstanding the parents will have an opinion about how the new home owners spend each and every dollar. The disapproving looks, the off handed comments and all the beating around the bush with questions about what and how the young couple spends their money. This puts a strain on everyone. The young couple starts to edit what they say around the parents as to avoid any potential conflict. They feel the need to hide the vacation they planned for fear of being judged. This once close family has been driven apart by the obligation, expectation and resentment of debt. A debt created in love with an unintended conscience.

I had a great friend that I grew up with since high school. He and I were in the same youth group from our sophomore year though our college and career years. Curtis and I spent summer nights toilet papering the homes of our friends and the days talking about which girls we liked.

Curtis was a groomsman in my wedding back in 1984. He was married not too long after that himself. He married a lovely girl we both knew from back in our youth group days. We all got busy with life and we drifted apart for a few years. One day Curtis called me out of the blue and told me he had kidney cancer. We reconnected for the time he had left. About eight months after Curtis passed, his wife asked to borrow some money. I gladly and foolishly lent her what she asked for. I say foolishly because if I had thought about it, I would have just given her the money. I never saw her or Curtis's kids again. She may not have been able to pay me back when she thought she could. She may have felt the need to avoid me. Maybe it was easier. If I had not made that loan, I could have kept my friend's family in my life. Remember the only debt you want to owe to those in your life you hold dear, is the debt of love.

> **"It's not how much you have, but how much you enjoy that makes happiness."**
> **Charles Spurgeon**

LAW #41

A little ink saves a lot of grief.

There is an old saying, "What the big print giveth, the little print taketh away." Read the fine print. Not many things will steal your happiness like making a bad deal. You need to make sure you understand all aspects of any agreement you enter into. Putting things in writing will keep agreements from shifting and changing with each person's recollection. No one wants to lose money in a deal gone bad, but you may lose something even more dearly if you don't spell out your agreements in writing with friends and family.

Many people think that if you are good friends with someone then you don't need to have agreements in writing. Well, I say the better the friend the more you need agreements to be in writing to ensure everyone knows the deal and no one misunderstands or forgets any part of it. It would be truly regrettable to lose a friend because of a faulty memory or due to some misperception in the details of an agreement. I should know because it happened to me.

About twenty-six years ago, I rented my home to friends of ours. We did not have a written agreement. Why would we need one? We were friends. Long story short, I thought I said they could rent it for a year and they thought I said it would be for two years. This misunderstanding could have been avoided with a contract. The friendship was never the same. Take it from me; the best mistakes are the ones you avoid.

"Each morning when I open my eyes; I, not events, have the power to make me happy or unhappy today. I can choose which it shall be. Yesterday is dead, tomorrow hasn't arrived yet. I have just one day, and I'm going to be happy in it."
Groucho Marx

LAW #42

Take a break. Change your scenery. Nothing can reenergize your body, mind and soul like a trip away.

"All work and no play..." It's not just a saying, it's a fact. Life is more interesting when we get away and change the pace of our lives even for a little while.

"But I can't spare the time; I have too much to do." It is easy for us to get so busy *doing* we can forget how to take the time to really live. (Now I sound like a hippie.) Look, life is short. Don't fall into the trap of putting off time spent with friends and family, having adventures or seeing and experiencing new things which can enrich your life, in order to keep some self-imposed schedule. You see, we all need fun and distraction in our life; a chance to reconnect with loved ones and to stop and take a breath. Isn't that why we work so hard, so that we are able to enjoy our lives, not merely endure them?

A number of years ago a study was done on what makes the highly successful among us so successful. When asked, "What is one of the top five things you attribute to your success?" 86% of those super achievers, surprisingly, responded saying, "Frequent trips away." They explained how their field of work was very competitive and they would take little weekend trips about once a month. This would help them recharge their batteries and give them time away from the day-to-day running of their business, in order to take a fresh look at things when they returned.

Life can be an adventure or a slow draining death. It's all how we approach it. If you want to find happiness then get out of town and see things, do things and have a little fun.

Remember, it's your life. Enjoy it!

"The moments of happiness we enjoy take us by surprise. It is not that we seize them, but that they seize us."   Ashley Montagu

LAW #43
Live below your means. Avoid credit and pay cash.

It's said, "a fool spends everything he makes, but a wise man saves something for a rainy day."

We live in a culture that wants us to buy, buy and buy some more. We're told it's good for the economy. However, we should learn to ask ourselves, "Is it good for *our* economy?" No!

The most common stress in life is over money. If you make $20,000 a year or $2,000,000 a year and you spend it all or worse, more than you make, you will have stress. Overspending is the equal opportunity thief of happiness. We all know that guy or girl who drives down the road in that great looking new car, wearing designer clothes, and living in that beautiful house around the corner, and still has the tan they got while on holiday in Hawaii. It is easy to envy them and want that lifestyle for ourselves. There is nothing wrong with having that lifestyle unless, as is so often the case, the car is leased, the clothes and the trip were bought with credit cards, and the house has a negative amortization loan, or has payments so high that if they hit any bump in life they run the risk of losing it.

I am in favor of having and doing nice things that you can afford. I am not in favor of financing your lifestyle; I want you to own it. Buying stuff with credit does two things.

1. It makes everything more expensive due to interest and   fees.
2. You are buying things for today with money you hope to
make tomorrow, promising your future away. You will not get ahead this way.

If you pay cash for what you buy you will think about it differently. It is too easy to swipe a card and spend more than you planned. I want you to control your money, not have your money have control over you.

Create a budget and think about where every dollar is going to be spent. Do you need to cut back; do you need to make more? A budget may be a dirty word to some of you but think of it like a map. You have to know where you are to see the path to where you want to go. Your goal is to spend a maximum of 90% of what you make and save at least 10% each month. This can be used to create an emergency fund so you will not have to borrow and go into debt when life happens. As you build that savings month after month and pay off old debt without getting into new debt, you will see how your life will feel lighter and you will no longer be at the mercy of the speed bumps of life.

"Don't wait around for other people to be happy for you. Any happiness you get you've got to make yourself."   Alice Walker

LAW #44

Be open to learn, but stay true to yourself while dealing with a critical world.

"Everyone's a critic." The ability to take constructive criticism is crucial to becoming a happier person. We grow more from our mistakes than we do from our accomplishments. Sometimes we are too close to a situation and can't see our part of what needs to change. This being said, we have to be very choosy of who we let comment on our life. Everyone has an opinion but not all opinions are equal. We have to be careful that the people we allow to criticize us have our best interest in mind. We all know people who pose as a concerned friend only to stir up trouble and increase our own insecurities. Learn to distinguish between the true friend and the saboteur in your life.

We all have things in our lives we need to change, but there are also things that make us unique, that make us, us. I know that I am not everyone's cup of tea and my wife, who knows me the best, is a saint. There are things about me that I like, that others would want to change. This is the same for most of us. We all have little idiosyncrasies that are unique to whom we are. For instance, I care more about dressing comfortably than looking fashionable.

That's one of mine, not the only one, but you get the idea.

Sometimes we need to hear the hard truth about things we need to change. We may have problems that affect our interactions with others that we are not aware of. It may be the things we say or what we do or how we do it. The truths that are hard to hear are also hard to tell you, and only a true friend will care enough to risk hurting you to help you. The bible says, "Blows from a friend are better than kisses from an enemy."

Avoid being defensive. We all have a tendency to feel attacked when our actions are called into question. Remember, if the person that's being critical of you loves you and only has your best interest in mind, take a beat and be willing to hear the words as a blessing to help you make the adjustments to become your very best.

> **"Future. The period of time in which our affairs prosper, our friends are true and our happiness is assured." Ambrose Bierce**

LAW #45

Do what is right, even when it's not easy. You will create a happiness you can live with.

Character is what you do when nobody is looking. There are a great many people who do not like themselves for one reason or another. We meet these people and think they are wonderful and can't understand why they have such a poor self-image. The truth is they know themselves better than we do. They know everything they have ever done, both good and bad as we all do. This knowledge will influence each of us in how we feel about ourselves. Even if we are the only one who knows our deeds, they will affect everything about us from how much money we make or feel we deserve to make, to who we pick as a mate.

When we do the right thing, no matter the cost, we can feel we are a man or woman of integrity, and that is priceless. If the teller at the bank or the cashier at the store gives us too much change and we keep it, our integrity is only worth that small amount of money. We could be bought or sold for that pittance. If we think of trading away our self worth for expediency we only cheat ourselves. These rules do not apply to sociopaths, but they do for most of us.

In short, be the person you want others to believe you are.

**"Life is a choice, it is your life. Choose consciously, choose wisely, choose honestly, choose happiness."
Bonnie Ware**

LAW #46

Your subconscious is always listening. Be careful what you tell it, it believes everything.

It has been called, "The Secret" or "The Law of Attraction," and is found in books like, *The Lazy Mans Way to Riches*. It is your subconscious. I know it sounds all new agey and metaphysical, but there really is something to it. Our subconscious is far more powerful than we may realize. Say you're at lunch with a friend and you are telling them about some actor in an old movie but you can't for the life of you remember the actor's name. You say,"it'll come to me" then you finish your lunch and go on your way. Later that night while you're getting ready for bed, in the middle of brushing your teeth you suddenly say, "Gary Cooper!" It finally came to you. That was your subconscious working on it. You gave it a task and like a computer program that runs in the background, your subconscious continues working on whatever problem you give it until it is resolved. This powerful subconscious works in each of us. It acts on whatever you tell it. Your subconscious does not distinguish between fact and sarcasm or false modesty, it believes everything you say. If you speak out loud the attributes you want to have as if you already posses them, you will start to create and manifest them within you. If you are consistent in what you say, both good and bad, it will happen. Do not say negative things about yourself, even if you are just fishing for compliments. Your subconscious will act to create that reality.

Your subconscious works on the things you tell it and ask it. It works to identify opportunities in the world around you that help to piece together the reality you seek. If you use your subconscious with purpose to help you and are aware of the power within you, how much faster will you be able to create the happy life you want?

"Happiness does not come from doing easy work but from the afterglow of satisfaction that comes after the achievement of a difficult task that demands our best." Theodore Rubin

LAW #47

Just like your mom said," Go outside and play."So fish, bike, surf, or camp, get out and enjoy the great outdoors!

Never have there been so many people so happy to be stuck inside. With TV, computers, and the internet, there are no shortages of things that keep us entertained without ever stepping foot outside. It may be time to unplug yourself from the electronic rat race around you and feel the warm vitamin D filled sun upon your pasty white face. We are a culture that is forgetting how to play outdoors. Playing can combine distraction from problems we can't control and exercise that strengthens our body and our immune system. It can also relieve stress we don't even know we carry. It often makes us physically tired enough to enjoy a good night's sleep. Playing in the unplugged world gives us the time we need for ourselves, freeing us from the tyranny of our electronic leash. Having fun, enjoying the fresh air and being out in the real world somehow helps put life into perspective. It does not have to be an active sport. It can be a walk along a treed path, or maybe a garden you like to putter in or perhaps a picnic in the park with a loved one. Playing outside helps us reconnect with ourselves. It reminds us of when we were young, when we were kids, when all things were possible.

Do I really have to convince you to go outside and play?

> "Happiness cannot be traveled to, owned, earned or worn. It is the spiritual experience of living every minute with love, grace and gratitude."
> Denis Waitley

LAW #48

Happiness is not complete when you don't know God. Don't fool yourself, there is a God and you need to know Him.

Okay, this is the last but not least truth for a reason. If I had made this the first law some of you would have put down the book and stopped reading before you got past the first page.

We all have a need to know Jesus. To know our Creator is what makes us look at the world with wonder. The moral code that tells us we have been wronged was put there by God. I believe there is a God sized hole in each of us that only God can fill. This does not stop people from trying to fill that hole with all sorts of other things. People use drugs, alcohol, sex, money, and all kinds of things to fill that hole in their lives. This will only leave them with an emptiness that will keep true happiness at bay. When we let The Lord fill that empty part of us that only He can fill, we find a peace and a feeling of completion in our life that's unmistakable.

If you already believe in God then seek Him, put Him first. If you don't believe then investigate for yourself, it's worth your time.

I have seen God work and witnessed miracles in my life, and I can confidently say that my life is a happier life by knowing Jesus Christ than it would be without Him. I encourage you to keep an open mind when it comes to God. Give Him a chance, and your happiest days are yet to come.

"Until now you have asked nothing in my name. Ask, and you will receive, that your joy may be full."
John 16: 24   (The Holy Bible)